The
Cloud Sign Miracle

A TRUE STORY OF A
MIRACULOUS ANSWER TO PRAYER

DAVID B. BLANCO

WESTBOW®
PRESS
A DIVISION OF THOMAS NELSON
& ZONDERVAN

Scripture taken from the Holy Bible, NEW INTERNATIONAL VERSION®. Copyright © 1973, 1978, 1984 by Biblica, Inc. All rights reserved worldwide. Used by permission. NEW INTERNATIONAL VERSION® and NIV® are registered trademarks of Biblica, Inc. Use of either trademark for the offering of goods or services requires the prior written consent of Biblica US, Inc.

WestBow Press books may be ordered through booksellers or by contacting:

WestBow Press
A Division of Thomas Nelson & Zondervan
1663 Liberty Drive
Bloomington, IN 47403
www.westbowpress.com
1 (866) 928-1240

Because of the dynamic nature of the Internet, any web addresses or links contained in this book may have changed since publication and may no longer be valid. The views expressed in this work are solely those of the author and do not necessarily reflect the views of the publisher, and the publisher hereby disclaims any responsibility for them.

Any people depicted in stock imagery provided by Thinkstock are models, and such images are being used for illustrative purposes only. Certain stock imagery © Thinkstock.

ISBN: 978-1-4908-7943-7 (sc)
ISBN: 978-1-4908-7944-4 (e)

Library of Congress Control Number: 2015907177

Print information available on the last page.

WestBow Press rev. date: 06/30/2015

TABLE OF CONTENTS

To

Susanne

My loving wife of 41 years,

An answer to prayer,

The most joyful person and

Believer I have ever known;

And to our children: Jonathan and Elizabeth

Who have supported both of us so faithfully in our

Days and hours of need

ACKNOWLEDGMENTS

Thanks to Sally who helped me end my loneliness, And provided companionship and sensible advice on the writing and Publishing of this book; Thanks to Bob Tuttle who gave me encouragement To proceed with this book after I retired, and taught Me that our God's will is perfect and ever refreshed. Thanks also to Reverend Bill MacDonald, Dr. Michael B. Brown, Dr. Mark Ralls and others for their insights and encouragement

INTRODUCTION

Jesus Christ taught His disciples certain sentences to pray when beginning to communicate with God. The words have become known as the Lord's Prayer.

> Our Father who art in heaven, Hallowed be thy name. Thy kingdom come; thy will be done on earth, as it is in heaven. Give us this day our daily bread, and forgive us our trespasses, as we forgive those who trespass against us. And lead us not into temptation, but deliver us from evil. For thine is the kingdom, the power and the glory, forever. Amen.

As a child, I memorized that prayer. I have prayed it thousands of times in churches and when commencing prayer on my own. When I prayed it slowly, I realized that much of the essence of the Christian faith was set forth in the prayer. When

I asked God ("Our Father who art in heaven") to listen to my prayers, I said this prayer.

He has listened to my prayers, responded to them, and answered them to help me many times during my life, including the time described in this book.

At a time of great indecision, turmoil, stress, and anxiety in my life, I asked God, after saying the Lord's Prayer, for a sign to help me with an important decision in my life. This book is about God's delivery of this sign to me. The sign was actually captured on film on my thirty-five millimeter camera (before digital cameras) in a way only God could accomplish—a beautiful and miraculous, loving way. This book is about some of the mysteries of this miraculous sign and my progress to date in discerning its teachings and meanings.

It is my hope that, with God's help, every person who considers the revelations in this book may be touched and inspired, as I have been, with the truth of God's love and the fact of His presence with us here in this part of His universe.

CHAPTER 1

"God Is in the Clouds"

It was early summer in 1993. I sat with my wife, Susanne, on a beautiful sandy beach on an island called the Bogue Banks, off the coast of North Carolina. We were on the south side of the island, with a broad view of the ocean and sky. In a tranquil and serene moment, I said, "God is in the clouds."

Susanne asked me what I meant. I explained—more than she wanted to know—that through the phenomenon of evaporation, established at the creation of the world, God has lifted fresh water from the salty ocean to form clouds. The winds have blown these clouds of water all over the world. The clouds let go of their fresh water upon arrival at their destination, and we call it rain. This process has continued for billions of years to grow the trees, plants, and rainforests that sustain life on earth. What a marvelous delivery system for providing life-giving water to humankind and the other animals and plants of God's creation that share the world with us. This is evidence of God's eternal and boundless love, which has created and sustained our blue planet. We should be so very grateful to God and be diligent stewards of this paradise God has provided.

Not until much later after that oceanfront conversation did I realize that during the more than four thousand years of biblical history, God and His angels have used rainclouds over the earth to send many messages to human beings. (See the list of biblical references at the end of this book.) In each case, these cloud signs and messages have been miraculous events that appear unexplainable by the laws of nature; they have been held to be supernatural in origin or an act of God. These are indeed signs and wonders of God's presence.

CHAPTER 2
Christian Upbringing

My mother and father took my sister and me to church regularly in our formative years, mostly to Centenary Methodist—a beautiful, large church in downtown Winston–Salem, North Carolina. We had moved there in 1950. For many years, my mother played the piano and led the singing in the large ladies' Sunday-school class (the Maude Williamson class) at this church. My mother was also active as a den mother for my age group when I was a Cub Scout; she was active as well in the Girl Scouts with my sister, Deanna. When I was growing up, my father was the leader of the Boy Scout troop affiliated with Centenary Methodist Church. I attended Sunday school at that church along with many other children, including twenty to thirty young boys from the local Methodist Children's Home, who arrived by bus.

In the Senior High Youth Fellowship at Centenary Methodist, I was fortunate to be led by a young Methodist youth leader named the Reverend Richard Hanner, who had been an Angier B. Duke scholar as an undergraduate at Duke University. He was also a graduate of Duke Divinity School. I looked up to Reverend Hanner, and I was blessed by his faithful obedience to God and Jesus Christ. I appreciated Reverend Hanner's spiritual nurture and leadership.

During those Senior High Youth Fellowship years, several ministers heavily influenced me to consider the idea of becoming a Methodist minister. These included Reverend Hanner and other senior Methodist pastors such as Dr. Mark Depp and Dr. Kenneth Goodson. Dr. Goodson later became a bishop of the Southern Methodist Church and taught homiletics and other religious courses at Duke Divinity School.

Partly because of these Methodist and Duke University connections, and partly because I was asked to compete for an Angier B. Duke Scholarship, I decided to attend Duke University for my college education after being accepted there.

Since childhood, I had heard and believed the message of Jesus Christ from many wonderful preachers, teachers, and witnesses to the reality of God, Jesus Christ, and the Holy Spirit. In an untold number of prayer sessions over my lifetime,

I always started with the Lord's Prayer, as Jesus taught us to pray (see Matthew 6:9–13). I had been very blessed in my life to receive answers to many prayers.

In college at Duke, I took Christian religion courses, but I really wanted to get a classical education in English and history. I decided to major in history. During my senior year, I wrote my history honors paper on the early development of the Uniform Code of Military Justice, based on some papers left to Duke University in its library. A North Carolina lawyer, who was elected to the US Congress after his service in World War I, had donated his papers to Duke University upon his death. I was directed by Professor Holly to open and study this large volume of papers for the first time. This member of Congress had been instrumental in establishing the Uniform Code of Military Justice, which became the American system of justice for our military in times of war and peace.

A law professor at Duke Law School, Professor Robinson Everett, an honor graduate of Harvard Law School, found out about my college paper and took an interest in it. He requested me to discuss the paper with him. In what was a fascinating hour for me in a brilliant law-school professor's office, Professor Everett was very complimentary about the research I had done and my honors paper itself. Professor Everett later served for a number of years as the chief judge of the US Military Court of Appeals.

As a young man in college, planning for my profession in life, I faced a difficult choice of either attending law school and becoming an attorney or else attending divinity school so as to become a minister of the gospel. My earthly father, David R. Blanco, encouraged me to become an attorney. He had a perception that law practice would give me a freedom to live where I wanted and decide what course to take for my life's work. On the other hand, as mentioned earlier, I was inspired by the encouragement I received from Reverend Hanner, Dr. Goodson, and other Methodist leaders to consider life in Christian ministry.

Based largely on the influence that my father's advice had upon me, I applied to and was accepted to law school at Duke University. I felt strongly that the law was a high calling and profession, as was life in the ministry. However, I chose law school and the legal profession and ended up practicing law for over forty years in North Carolina. I was very satisfied with that profession for my life's work.

CHAPTER 3

Christian Adulthood

After I had graduated from Duke University Law School, I passed the North Carolina bar examination in 1966. I soon realized that there was only a limited job market for positions in law practice—even for a graduate from one of the top law schools in the country. I ended up taking a position as a law clerk to a US District Court judge in the Middle District of North Carolina—Judge Eugene Gordon. I served as one of his two law clerks for two years: from August 1966 until August 1968. Clerking for a federal judge was an informative and helpful experience for a young law graduate. Judge Gordon was a wonderful lawyer from Burlington, North Carolina, who had also attended Duke Law School. He was definitely a fine

Christian gentleman as well as an astute scholar in federal and North Carolina law.

When the clerkship ended, I searched again for a law-practice position in the Winston–Salem area. Receiving offers from two smaller law firms, I decided I did not want that type of practice; I took a position with Wachovia Bank in their trust department in August 1968. Wachovia had one of the most highly rated trust departments in the Southeast. I worked there for about three years. Then I was offered a legal position in the Wachovia Mortgage Company because I had asked to be notified if legal jobs came up throughout the Wachovia Bank system. I took a job in that area of the bank, assisting with the Wachovia Real Estate Investment Trust management. I learned a good deal about the legal work involved in commercial real estate transactions and related lending. That work concluded upon my receiving an offer to practice law (commencing on January 15, 1973) with a Duke Law School classmate.

I was happily engaged in the practice of law from that date in January 1973 and throughout my career, concentrating in whatever area was called for as we built the law firm from two lawyers to about twenty lawyers by 1993. I principally concentrated in trusts and estates, commercial real estate, mergers and acquisitions, corporate governance, and securities law.

Once I had settled back in Winston–Salem after college and law school, I began teaching Sunday school to senior high school students at Centenary Methodist Church. I did that teaching for several years.

In 1969, I married Susanne Hall in a small Episcopal church in South Carolina. She had joined that church with her parents, sisters, and brother.

We attended Centenary Church in Winston–Salem for several years, but it was just too large for Susanne. We joined St. Paul's Episcopal Church in Winston–Salem as a compromise, and our son was baptized there in 1973. After enjoying that church for several years, we were led to attend First Presbyterian Church, where we joined and then stayed for the next twenty-five years. Our daughter was baptized in that church in 1979. Both Susanne and I served as deacons at First Presbyterian Church, and I was later elected to the board of elders (the session) for two terms there. I was also blessed to serve in the formation of their men's ministry, which grew to routinely having about seventy men attending its breakfast meetings and other functions. This ministry helped develop a more active group of men in the leadership of that church. (The women were already quite active in the church.)

Eventually, another young elder and I started and led a small Bible study group for men, which lasted about ten years.

My faith in Jesus Christ—and belief that He was who He said He was—continued to grow. In addition, my prayer life grew more regular. And my relationship with my heavenly

Father and the Holy Spirit seemed to grow more personal. I often prayed about the lawyers and staff people in our law firm, and I received many answers to my prayers to love and care for them. I tried to demonstrate Christian love in my daily contacts with the lawyers and our wonderful staff of nonlawyers.

In 1988, I assumed more of the leadership of our law firm, while also developing a very active practice of law. I continued these activities for about the next fifteen years. It was during this time that I asked for a sign from God about what to do with the law firm and in my own life. As I discuss later in this book, I received the sign, which was in the form of a large *crown* shape in the clouds.

CHAPTER 4

Indecision, Stress, Worry, and Anxiety

In the early nineties, while I continued in the law practice, I served on the Winston–Salem board of directors for Southern National Bank. In that capacity, I assisted in the board's effort to convince the Southern National Bank to move its headquarters from Lumberton, North Carolina, to Winston–Salem. We sought to make such a move attractive by submitting a plan to assist in raising millions of dollars in deposit pledges if the bank would relocate its headquarters to our city. This effort was successful, and Southern National Bank agreed to move its headquarters to the city.

Later, as a part of that growing relationship with Southern National Bank, I received an offer by the bank's president to move our law firm to its proposed new regional bank building at the five-points intersection in Winston–Salem, where our firm would lease some space.

I presented this offer to our law firm's board of directors and received their approval to pursue the matter. Many of the partners thought that such a deal with the bank should be conditioned upon finding a purchaser for the building where we were currently located and completing that sale. (The building was owned by many of the firm's board members.) I continued to press for our law firm to make a firm commitment that was without condition.

A number of the firm members were unsure that we should risk moving to a new office building, particularly because our most senior attorney had resigned from the firm in April 1994 to form a new law firm. Some of our firm's board members were unsure as to how many clients the departing attorney would take with him.

Being president of the law firm and chairman of its board of directors, as well as a husband and a father of young growing children, I believed that determining the direction in which I should lead the law firm was of critical importance.

These issues were causing me a great deal of stress and anxiety. Should our law firm stay where we were or take the many risks to move to a new location? Would our law firm retain all of our attorneys and partners and most of the legal work and clients that we had developed, or would there be some decline in our attorneys as well as the clientele we had developed? I, of course, could not see into the future, and I was uncertain about which path to follow.

I had often prayed about matters and asked for direction from God in prayer. I believed that I had received serenity, peace, and a sense of direction in those events. Susanne and I talked a good deal about the issues that I currently faced, and she recommended that I pray about it and ask God for direction.

CHAPTER 5

My Prayer for a Sign

Sometime in the spring or early summer of 1995, in a fervent plea to God, after saying the Lord's Prayer, I asked God for a *sign*. I sought a *sign* for direction in my life and to alleviate the stress, worry, and anxiety I was experiencing. I wanted to be at peace. I knew the business decision could greatly affect my family, the attorneys and staff of our law firm, and their families, about 150 people all told. In earlier prayers I had sensed or received direction that I should spend more time loving and caring for all these human beings. God's love and leading in retrospect.

The prayer I prayed is the one given by Jesus when He preached to the crowds in the Sermon on the Mount, as set forth in Matthew 6:9-13 (KJV).

9. This then is how you should pray: "Our Father who art in heaven,

Hallowed be thy name.

10. Thy kingdom come,

Thy will be done,

On earth as it is in heaven.

11. Give us this day our daily bread;

12. And forgive us our debts,

as we forgive our debtors.

13. And lead us not into temptation,

but deliver us from evil:

For thine is the kingdom,

And the power, and the glory, forever.

Amen."

CHAPTER 6

A Beautiful Part of God's Creation

Later in July of 1995, Susanne and I returned to the beach with our children and close friends and their children, seeking rest and rejuvenation. My wife and I had discovered that we could find rest and peace at this island beach off of the coast of North Carolina. It was a lovely spot with sand dunes, twenty-five feet high, deposited by the ocean over many years. Beyond the high dunes on the inland side were numerous lovely old oak trees, commonly called sea oaks, many of which had large trunks and branches.

Theodore Roosevelt, our twenty-sixth president of the United States, had reputedly bought this tract of land at the turn of the twentieth century for use as a hunting and fishing preserve. His children and grandchildren had recently developed the land in an environmentally careful way.

This beautiful spot had been created by years of the ocean pounding the seashells into soft, white sand and piling up these high sand dunes. Out of the dunes grew natural sea oats (a tall grass) and other vegetation. These plants held the dunes in place, allowing the large sea oak trees to thrive right behind the sand dunes. A beautiful part of God's creation!

CHAPTER 7

My Photographs of Dunes, Ocean, Sky and Clouds

After a wonderful July, 1995 beach vacation, we were near the end of a weeklong stay at the beach with our family and friends. My thirty-five millimeter camera was out on the balcony railing of our beachfront cottage, waiting for me to take pictures on the last night of our stay. It was our habit to take these pictures just as the sun was setting, to capture the pink and gold glow of the sunsets at the beach. It was a gorgeous early evening, with fluffy white cumulus clouds forming and drifting by. It was warm, but there was a cool, light breeze off the ocean.

Susanne came out onto the balcony where I was sitting with my friend and said, "Davey, take some pictures of the sea oats and clouds so we can remember them when we get home."

I started snapping pictures. Facing south, I took four or five photographs with the sea oats appearing at the bottom of each frame, growing out of the top of the dunes, while the rest of the frame was filled by the ocean beyond and the clouds.

When I returned home and developed the film, there were two photographs of much interest: (1) a picture of a cloud forming and moving into view, and (2) in the final shot, a beautiful large cloud in the shape of a massive *crown.* The cloud, viewed to the south, glowed in the light of the sun setting in the west.

Had I not started snapping pictures when Susanne told me to take the pictures, I would have missed these two amazing photographs.

For some reason, the large cloud in the shape of a crown was centered perfectly in the frame of the photograph, although I had not consciously tried to center it.

Here are copies of the last two intriguing photographs I took that evening:

Angel at Work on the Cloud Sign

Cloud Sign Complete

Did the Final Photograph Contain the Sign I Had Asked for in Prayer? If So, What Was Its Message?

As I looked for the first time at the three-by-four-inch developed prints, in the second-to-last shot I saw a cloud seemingly starting to form a particular shape—but it was not complete. Then, in the final photograph in the series, that cloud had taken the shape of a large crown. (From now on, I will refer to the cloud shown in the final photograph as *the Cloud Sign*.) There were also other forms and shapes in the Cloud Sign that I could not see clearly or understand. I went back to the film developer and had larger, eight-by-ten-inch prints made from the negatives so that I could have a better look at the details.

One day soon afterward, I took a copy of the larger prints of the final two photographs to show to a friend who was a young minister at our church. We met for lunch, and I asked him for his understanding of the photographs. After looking at the final photograph, he said that in his opinion it was indeed a *sign* in answer to my prayer for a sign about the direction to take in my life. I asked what he thought the message of the Cloud Sign was. He said he believed it was to remind me of the words of advice from Jesus Christ presented in the Sermon on the Mount in Matthew 6:33 (KJV): *"Seek ye first the kingdom of God and his righteousness; and all these things shall be added unto you."*

That night, I went to my Bible and carefully read again the Sermon on the Mount from the gospel of Matthew. I studied these passages then and for many days and months to follow. Over time, I became convinced that I had received the sign I had prayed for. It was a miraculous, God-given response to my prayer. Having reached this conclusion, I was incredibly humbled indeed that God had listened to my prayer and in the person of the Holy Spirit had answered it in such a beautiful and miraculous way. Each human being is a child of God. Each physical human body is made up of atoms from God's universe that were created over the course of billions of years. God has put incredible, unfathomable effort into us—all of us, His children. Each person is supremely important and very loved!

In the Sermon on the Mount, Jesus advises us about worry and anxiety and gives us godly advice about what is important in our earthly life; this sermon is shown in chapters 5 through 7 of the gospel of Matthew.

Consider this passage from Matthew 6:19–34 (NIV) (the added emphasis is mine):

Treasures in Heaven

19. Do not store up for yourselves treasures on earth, where moth and rust destroy, and where thieves break in and steal.

20. But store up for yourselves treasures in heaven, where moth and rust do not destroy, and where thieves do not break in and steal.

21. For where your treasure is, there your heart will be also.

22. The eye is the lamp of the body. If your eyes are good, your whole body will be full of light.

23. But if your eyes are bad, your whole body will be full of darkness. If then the light within you is darkness, how great is that darkness!

24. No one can serve two masters. Either he will hate the one and love the other, or he will be devoted to the one and despise the other. **You cannot serve both God and Money.**
Do not worry.

25. Therefore I tell you, do not worry about your life, what you will eat or drink; or about your body, what you will wear. Is not life more important than food, and the body more important than clothes?

26. Look at the birds of the air; they do not sow or reap or store away in barns, and yet your heavenly Father feeds them. Are you not much more valuable that they?

27. Who of you by worrying can add a single hour to his life?

28. And why do you worry about clothes? See how the lilies of the field grow. They do not labor or spin.

29. Yet I tell you that not even Solomon in all his splendor was dressed like one of these.

30. If that is how God clothes the grass of the field, which is here and tomorrow is thrown into the fire, will he not much more clothe you, O you of little faith?

31. So do not worry, saying, "What shall we eat?" or "What shall we drink?" or "What shall we wear?"

32. For the pagans run after all these things, and your heavenly Father knows that you need them.

33. But seek first his kingdom and his righteousness, and all these things will be given to you as well.

34. Therefore do not worry about tomorrow, for tomorrow will worry about itself. Each day has enough trouble of its own.

CHAPTER 9

Coming to Comprehend and Grasp More Fully the Mysteries and Messages of the Miraculous Sign

I have come to believe that this sign in the clouds was a sign and a wonder, a miracle, a rare glimpse of an angel. It was also a revelation from God, our Christian God, full of the mystery and complexity of our God. It is a miracle because it was not just an accident of nature but instead was purposely created by an angel of God in answer to a prayer. The angel appeared long enough to prepare the sign in the clouds in the form of a large crown and then disappeared.

I believe that my young minister friend was right—that it was a *sign* in answer to my prayers to God for direction. I believe that it was a message or sign from God in the person of the Holy Spirit, to remind me (us) of Jesus' words, through the supernatural power of one of God's angels. I believe it is miraculous that this angel was able to form a cloud of vapor in the precise location where it was needed, in order to be photographed by me. It was miraculous that the angel could create this cloud in the shape of a large, regal crown at the precise moment I was to snap a picture, thus surely delivering the wonderful Cloud Sign message to me.

I had questions galore. Did the Holy Spirit cause Susanne to ask me to take the photographs at that precise moment? Or did the Holy Spirit, knowing in advance when Susanne would be requesting photographs, set the angel to work exactly at the right time in order to deliver the photograph to me (us!) upon the final camera click?

My young friend said that God, Jesus, and the Holy Spirit were reminding me and others of Jesus Christ's admonitions or guidance about storing up treasures in heaven rather than on earth. Furthermore, the message to me was not to worry about these things I was worrying about, but rather to "seek first the Kingdom of God and His righteousness, and all these other things will be given to you as well."

Later, I realized that the gospel of Luke presents teachings of Jesus Christ that are similar to those recorded in Matthew. See Luke 12:22–34.

I continued to study the Cloud Sign. I found opportunities to further seek the kingdom of God by supporting my church, First Presbyterian Church. Having served as a deacon, I was called to become an elder. I accepted the post, which lasted for several years. I became more involved in the personnel, finance, and other administrative committees of the church and in the new men's ministry. I started performing legal work for First Presbyterian (mostly pro bono) in an active growth phase for the church, in which the church purchased nearby real estate upon which to build a new worship center.

In regard to my understanding of the mysteries of the Cloud Sign photograph, I had started on what was effectively a long pilgrimage to study and comprehend more fully the apparently miraculous sign and its wonders. As I studied, I realized that some of Jesus Christ's prophecies and teachings were depicted in the Cloud Sign, some nineteen and a half centuries after Jesus Christ revealed these truths to us human beings, children of God. There were still many mysteries in the Cloud Sign I did not comprehend.

Why was the Cloud Sign in the shape of a massive Crown?

We all have sung the Hymn which commands that we: "Bring forth the Royal Diadem and Crown him Lord of all!" but did most of us realize that there are 38 references to crowns, crowns of glory , crowns of thorns, etc in the Bible? See Appendix at the end of the book. We all know that Crowns are used to recognize Kings and signify Kingdoms in scripture and in England and other countries with Kings and kingdoms.

Moreover, I was not certain what I should do with this miraculous sign that I had been given. I felt unworthy to tell this story. Thus, I had copies made of the photographs and I put the negatives in our bank lockbox in an attempt to preserve them. I also had the last photograph enlarged as much as I could; I placed this on a poster board so I could show it to my ministers, to fellow church elders, and to other Christian friends. I have shown that enlargement of the Cloud Sign to all senior ministers of the churches I attended since I received the sign: initially, First Presbyterian Church, and later, Centenary United Methodist Church in the same city.

The Face at the Top Left of the Cloud Is a Miraculous Image within the Final Cloud Sign Photo

At a worship service one Sunday morning at First Presbyterian Church, I received the discernment that it is the face of Jesus Christ which is located at the top left of the crown cloud. It is depicted as a face of clear skin with deep-set or dark eyes. My discernment occurred when the congregation and I recited the Apostle's Creed in that service. Here is part of that creed:

> … On the third day he rose from the dead and ascended into Heaven *and sitteth on the right hand of God, the Father Almighty; from thence He shall come to judge the living and the dead* (from a translation of the *Didache*, a book of early Christian teachings, in *Book of Worship United Methodist Hymnal*) (emphasis added).

Suddenly, I realized that from the perspective of someone looking at the Cloud Sign or the photograph of it, this face was on the top *left* side of the crown. But from God's or the angel's perspective, the face was on the top *right* part of the crown; thus, that face in the cloud was depicted to be on the right side of the crown, or the right hand of God. It was on our *left* hand, but on His *right* hand—***in the place of highest honor!***

33

I Believe the Face Depicted Is Christ's Face

The face at the top left of the crown is the face of a human being *who has been resurrected from this earth, lifted into God's kingdom, and is present with God and His angels.* The face is shown in the Cloud Sign in the position of highest honor—near the top of the crown at the right hand of God. The face is nonjudgmental; with no hint of prejudgment. *Jesus is not depicted in the Cloud Sign prejudging us, because He loves and understands us, having taken on a human body Himself. He is giving us who live now the freedom to make our choices during our respective lives on this earth, with no coercion.*

In the next-to-last photograph of that eventful evening, the face which, as I refer to it, is being "worked on by the angel" seems to be a more severe face, with a heavy brow, full of judgment. In contrast, the final face in the last photograph (the completed Cloud Sign) is not judgmental, and it has been lifted *higher* up on the Cloud Sign, in the highest place of honor.

I had questions whether the dark, deep-set eyes, or what appeared to be "sunglasses," could be a depiction of coins over the eyes of Jesus. (This derives from a preexisting theory of some people that a burial custom at the time of Jesus was to place coins over the eyelids of the deceased.) Or is there another meaning? I do not have an answer yet, but I am certain that the resurrected, glorified Jesus Christ can now see all things totally clearly. He is a part of God's kingdom: in the place of highest honor; all seeing; all knowing; omniscient; eternal; a part of heaven; a Person of the Trinity; holding the power and glory of God.

God Is Light

There was a great deal of reflected light proceeding from this one cloud, a light which crossed the ocean toward me in "broad daylight," about five o'clock on a July afternoon. The light came straight at my camera (and at my eye). The light of God was presented to my eye; God was attempting to *fill me with light.*

Who Crafted the Cloud Sign? Was It an Angel of the Lord? Was It a Seraphim?

I went to the Christian bookstore and bought all the books they had on angels in the Bible. I was trying to comprehend how— in answer to a prayer lifted to heaven by a human being—a spiritual creature from heaven could contrive a distinctive cloud, imbued with mysteries. It was a cloud that we could see then and study later as well. How could this angel cause a depiction of a face at the top left (at the right hand of God)? How could the angel have all this completed with perfect timing so that my camera caught it exactly at the right moment after my wife, a human being, asked me to take some pictures? This Cloud Sign delivery was a supernatural event not possible to humans but possible to an angel of God on behalf of God the Father, His Son Jesus Christ, and the Holy Spirit.

In the middle of the huge cloud's crown shape (in the last photograph) is a shadowy figure that appears to be a birdlike creature. It has a rounded head with two eyes looking straight out at me and my camera, and it appears to have six wings (three short wings on each side) which are all opened.

Much later I discovered a description of a *seraphim* or *seraph* in Isaiah 6:1–(NIV):

> 6 In the year that King Uzziah died, I saw the Lord seated on a throne, high and exalted, and the train of his robe filled the temple. Above him were seraphs, each with six wings: With two wings they covered their faces, with two they covered their feet, and with two they were flying. And they were calling to one another:
>
> "Holy, holy, holy is the LORD Almighty, The whole earth is full of his glory."
>
> At the sound of their voices the doorposts and thresholds shook and the temple was filled with smoke.

"Woe to me" I cried. "I am ruined! For I am a man of unclean lips, and I live among a people of unclean lips, and my eyes have seen the King, the LORD Almighty."

Then one of the seraphs flew to me with a live coal in his hand, which he had taken with tongs from the altar. With it he touched my mouth and said, "See, this has touched your lips, your guilt is taken away and your sin atoned for."

In the *NIV Study Bible* (Zondervan 1985), a footnote for verse 2 of this chapter of Isaiah states that seraphs are "angelic beings not mentioned elsewhere. The Hebrew root underlying this word means 'burn,' perhaps to indicate their purity as God's ministers ... they correspond to the 'living creatures' of Rev. 4:6–9, each of whom also had six wings."

I looked at the film negative of the second-to-last frame and the corresponding print. There, it appears that the seraphim angel is turned around, facing away from me, with the back of the angel's head toward me and the camera. The angel appears to be working on the cloud with something that looks like a baton. The seraphim angel appears to be creating or producing the cloud itself. But the ultimate Cloud Sign picture, taken only a matter of seconds later, shows the seraphim angel turned around, looking right at me and the camera, as if to say, "Behold!

There—you have the *sign* you prayed for and your answer to prayer. I have delivered God's message!"

Wow! What a miraculous answer to prayer! A human being, a child of God, prayed for a sign in the midst of indecision, worry, and anxiety, asking for direction and peace in his life. And God, with the help of one of His angels, answered that prayer with a miraculous sign. God's advice to me appears to be, among other advice, to *seek first the kingdom of God* and God's righteousness and all the worries, anxieties, and turmoil would be resolved, and I would be provided for, as would my loved ones. This advice put me at ease and at peace, not only to continue serving God as a layperson in my church, but also to continue service to my fellow man as an attorney practicing my profession. This Godly advice helped me to put the law firm issues in proper perspective and eliminated the anxiety about the decision for myself and our attorneys and staff whom I cared about deeply. I was made to be at peace about the direction of my life for the time being, which was important given what was coming in a few years because of my wife Susanne's illness.

There Were Further Revelations

There was a second *face* in the Cloud Sign, at the bottom right. This face appeared to be looking west, as the Cloud Sign was facing due north toward the camera. I wondered whether this face could be a depiction of Saint Paul, who was led by Jesus to take the good news of Christianity to the Gentiles (including my ancestors, the Pilgrims, millions of others, and me) who were then and later mostly located to the *west* of Jerusalem. Paul took the message all the way to Rome and it spread throughout the Roman empire, which was mostly located west of the Holy Land.

There seem to be other faces or profiles of faces looking out of the cloud toward the east and west. One can clearly make out human profiles of a nose, a mouth, a chin. Whom do they depict? Are they representative of other saints who are part of God's kingdom?

There was something else portrayed coming out of the *mouth* of the face on the bottom right of the Cloud Sign; this additional mysterious feature extends halfway across the sign just under the feet of the angel. I did not understand whether the additional feature was a depiction of other revelations by this angel in the Cloud Sign. I present more discussion of that possible revelation later.

Our Trip to Ephesus and Istanbul in 1999

Susanne and I, with some close friends, traveled in 1999 to Athens, Greece, and from there to Turkey, where we visited Istanbul as well as the site of the ancient city of Ephesus. Prior to this trip, I prayed to the Lord that He make something good come out of the trip and that it would not just be a pleasure trip. I had no idea that a significant discernment would be presented to me in Istanbul.

We visited the huge cathedral in Istanbul known as the Hagia Sophia. Translated, that means "The Church of the Holy Wisdom." This massive cathedral is a former Christian cathedral, originally built by the Roman Emperor Constantine, which had been destroyed but was finally rebuilt in about AD 562—some 1,434 years before the Cloud Sign photograph. Later in the building's history, it was converted to an Ottoman mosque.

Inside the cathedral I was amazed to observe what appeared to be a massive depiction of a seraphim angel, presented in gold mosaic on the flying buttress support structure high above the floor of the massive cathedral. This seraphim angel looked very much like the angel in my Cloud Sign photograph who appeared to have prepared the Cloud Sign. Here is the photograph I took of this seraphim angel in the Hagia Sophia:

Seraphim Angel on Hagia Sophia Ceiling

The seraphim angel depicted on the ceiling had a large, round, birdlike head with two eyes peering out as from coals of fire and six small wings, three on each side of the seraphim. The seraphim, in gold mosaic form, was created sometime around AD 537 to 562, more than fourteen centuries earlier, by someone who had read about seraphim angels in Scripture, possibly in Isaiah or Revelation. The seraphim angel in the photograph of the Cloud Sign looked very much like the seraphim angel depicted on the ceiling of the cathedral. Since seraphim angels are mentioned in Old Testament Scripture, it would appear that they may be thousands of years old.

Back at home, I studied the books on angels and realized that seraphim angels have been messengers for God that were described in both the Old and New Testaments in many places. So they have been bringing messages to human beings for thousands of years! Some descriptions of angels might be helpful to those reading this book.

> I am convinced that these heavenly beings exist and that they provide unseen aid on our behalf. I also believe in Angels because I have sensed their presence in my life on special occasions … When Christians die, an Angel will be there to comfort us, to give us peace and joy at that most critical hour and usher us

into the presence of God whom we shall dwell with forever.

—Billy Graham, Evangelist
Angels: God's Secret Agents (1975)

Of course, some people will say Angels don't exist, never having seen one. And other people will ask why they appear only to certain humans. Others will say that Angels come to everyone. The question is who will recognize them when they come?

—Sophy Burnham, *A Book of Angels* (1992)

Angels are creations of God, and under the direction of the Holy Spirit they help us carry out our assignments as believers.

—Terry Law, *The Truth about Angels* (1994)

Angels, then, are real. Angels are spiritual beings, godlike but not God. Nor are they human — though they may appear in human form — they are immortal.

—Larry Kinnaman, *Angels Light and Dark* (1994)

Angels are the dispensers and the administrators of the Divine beneficence towards us; they regard our safety, undertake our defense, direct our ways and exercise solicitude that no evil befall us … God does not make angels the ministers of His power and goodness in order to divide His glory with them, so neither does He promise His assistance in their ministry, that we may divide our confidence between them and Him.

—John Calvin, Protestant Reformer
Institutes of Religions, Book 1, Chapter 4 (1536)

Angels have manifested themselves to men and women though vision, hearing and feeling. Why then should we consider them purely immortal substance having no connection with the visible universe? *Our knowledge of Angels leads us to believe they are connected with the world of matter.* [Indeed!] (emphasis added)

—Thomas Timpson, *Angel of God* (1845)

I came to know that these words were true and that angels are still performing God's service today because in my prayer to God, I had asked Him to give me a sign, to give me direction and peace. And apparently He dispatched an angel to convey the sign. Angels are still being used by God today to send messages to us.

Later I had lunch with Jim Johnson, PhD, a wonderful Christian, teacher, and leader in the Presbyterian Church. I showed him the Cloud Sign picture and told him the story. Jim is a highly trained scientist at Bowman Gray School of Medicine, Wake Forest University, which is a medical and biomedical research hospital. He is a knowledgeable Christian scholar and teacher. Jim commented that the cloud was probably about a thousand feet high and was out several thousand feet from the beach. This distance was far enough away for the camera to capture the entire Cloud Sign. He said that the angel figure is huge as well, probably several hundred feet tall. Jim believed that it was a gift from God to me in answer to a fervent prayer.

I asked Jim whether he thought the sign should be shown to others and whether the story should be told more broadly than only to the local ministers and devout Christians whom I knew. He answered that he felt it was a gift from God just for me, my family, and my loved ones and that there was no duty to disclose this to anyone. Jim told me that God does not need to prove His existence to anyone; God simply loves me and wants me to seek His kingdom and His righteousness.

CHAPTER 10
"Tell the Story"

In later prayer about this matter and whether I should do something further with the photographs and with the Cloud Sign, I heard a still, small voice say: "Tell the story." That simple! But how best to do that, given my busy law practice? Also, later, there were nine years of caring for my dear wife during her long illness with Alzheimer's disease.

On this matter, it helps to read two related parables of Jesus: the parable which the NIV Study Bible labels as "Salt and Light" and the parable it labels as "A Lamp on a Stand."

In Matthew 5:14, Jesus says, "You are the light of the world. A city on a hill cannot be hidden. Neither do people light a lamp and put it under a bowl. Instead they put it on its stand and it gives light to everyone in the house. In the same way, let your light shine before men, that they may see your good deeds and praise your Father in Heaven."

And in Mark 4:21–23, Jesus says, "Do you bring in a lamp to put it under a bowl or a bed? Instead, don't you put it on its stand? For whatever is hidden is meant to be disclosed, and whatever is concealed is meant to be brought out into the open. If anyone has ears to hear, let them hear."

I believe that once God gives a direction to humans, He does not change His mind. His words are not taken back. His words are unchanging and forever—unlike the words of human beings.

I picked up my efforts to tell the story and told it to more people, including most of the ministers of the two churches we attended during this period. I also told the story to the person who started the Master's Loft chain of religious bookstores. He was very touched by the witness and told me it made the hair on the back of his neck stand on end. I gave him a copy of the Cloud Sign photograph.

I showed a copy of the Cloud Sign photograph to my head minister at the Presbyterian church, and I also have shown it to other ministers at that church.

I showed it on several occasions to the men's Bible study group of ten or twelve men that I had started with another elder at the Presbyterian church some years ago.

I showed it to our friends from Houston and other Christians that we knew and with whom we associated.

Also, I invited to lunch the head minister of the large Methodist church we now attend. I gave him a copy of the Cloud Sign photograph and an early version of this manuscript. He thought that the image coming out of the mouth of the face on the bottom right of the Cloud Sign looked like Jesus standing in the back of the boat on the sea of Galilee with His disciples. Jesus is shown quieting the storm and their fears. My friend said this was an image of peace and of the divine power of Christ over the elements on this earth; it brought calm and peace to His disciples to know that Jesus was able to calm and control the seas and the wind. Jesus probably was involved as well in giving me calm and peace by virtue of the delivery of this Cloud Sign to me.

CHAPTER 11

A Loving Answer to Prayer

I am convinced that this Cloud Sign was a perfectly beautiful and loving answer to prayer. It was at the same time all of the following:

- Totally loving to me, because it was a response to my prayer in a loving way, as a father might respond to a son who is troubled and needs direction.
- Responsive to the prayer I lifted up—but it was so much more than I could grasp at the time.
- Kind and gentle.
- Magnificent.
- Full of light and goodness.
- Full of mystery.

- Serene, quiet, and peaceful.
- A multifaceted admonition: to seek first God's kingdom; that God is King and should be Lord of my life; that I should seek His righteousness—His lack of sin, His love, His mercy, His kindness, His justice, His peace—and all these other things asked for would be granted unto me as well.

CHAPTER 12

The Angel of God Created a Sign Out of the Water— Full of Light and Truth

How did the angel create this sign? My answer is: I do not know. It is clear that this angel knew I had asked for a sign. There had been a communication from the Holy Spirit to the angel, and that angel picked a moment to present this sign to me when my camera was ready and my wife would ask me to photograph the sea oats.

The timing was absolutely perfect, because I had no idea that this cloud was there; I would have missed the sign entirely but for the photograph. Furthermore, the timing by which the cloud was centered in the frame of my camera at the precise moment the angel finished the Cloud Sign is more than an incredible happenstance.

It is clear that the angel could bring the elements of the fresh water into the white cloud and form the cloud and keep the cloud together, creating the images in the cloud and reflecting in our direction the light from the setting sun to the west. To have all this done at precisely the right moment, knowing that I would click the camera at that moment, is miraculous.

I believe that God, in the person of the Holy Spirit, also had something to do with my wife coming out and telling me precisely at the right moment, "Davey, take some pictures of the sea oats and clouds so we can remember them when we get home." God used my wife to assist in making sure that I saw the sign, as I was about to miss it!

So now, after all this, I am passing on to you, the reader, this message, so you do not miss it either.

CHAPTER 13
A Personal Testimony

All the events described in this book actually happened, and the photographs are real. I truly believe that the Lord God Almighty sent an angel to present a sign in answer to my prayer. These things are true and proven to me to my satisfaction by the legal standards with which I am familiar: "by the greater weight of the evidence" and "beyond a reasonable doubt." I can even go so far as to say these things are true "beyond a *shadow* of a doubt" to me. And in the midst of a later prayer, I heard a still, small voice (perhaps the Holy Spirit) say to me: "Tell the story." That is what I am doing, with the Lord's help.

I hope others who read this book will be inspired by the truth of God's presence with us. God and His angels are alive, still with us, and helping us on this earth with our needs, both spiritual and material. God is giving us guidance to seek our salvation. We only have to ask God, Jesus, or the Holy Spirit. In Luke 11:9–13 (NIV), Jesus said, "So, I say to you: Ask and it will be given to you; seek and you will find; knock and the door will be opened to you. For everyone who asks receives: he who seeks finds: and to him who knocks, the door will be opened. Which of you fathers, if your son asks for a fish, will give him a snake instead? Or if he asks for an egg, will give him a scorpion? If you then, though you are evil, know how to give good gifts to your children, how much more will your Father in heaven give the Holy Spirit to those who ask Him!"

Know that God loves us very much and that His Holy Scriptures are truthful. Know that what Jesus Christ said while He was on earth was true then and is true today. Know that His Word leads to life abundant on this earth and to life eternal in heaven or other realms. Know that we just need to follow Christ's commandments to love the Lord our God with all our heart, soul, mind, and spirit, and to love our neighbors as ourselves.

- God has not given up on us.
- He is here with us, helping us.
- He is loving us with daily bread.
- He forgives us our trespasses as we forgive those who trespass against us.
- God answers our prayers prayed in Christ's name.

May we all heed the Lord's admonitions and seek first the kingdom of God and His righteousness; God will provide for all our needs. He will give us life abundant in this life and the life everlasting. That is the message of the Cloud Sign.

The Cloud Sign, the related photographs, and God's leading me in discernment of His messages comprise a miraculous revelation that the God I pray to is still there. He is alive. He has great power in this world and, I believe, in the next—in heaven. He answers the prayers of human beings as He did for me. We only need to ask, seek or knock!

What is man that God is mindful of him? God has invested incalculable energy and creative power into His creation of human beings and His creation of our beautiful blue planet. We owe our lives to God, as well as the lives of our forefathers and mothers, our children, grandchildren, and all those to come before the "end of the age." God very lovingly created all of us. We have a purpose to be God's stewards of this earth— including its creatures—as well as to take God's Word to the world and all its people. God's Word is true and has been (and continues to be) revealed to us as we and others have lived on this earth.

A final testimony to add here is that My dear wife of 41 years, Susanne Hall Blanco, began to exhibit signs of dementia in 2001, at the age of 55 years. She was diagnosed with Alzheimer's disease in 2004 and suffered the inevitable deterioration of her mental and physical capacities for almost 10 years before her death from these ravages in December 2010.

The Cloud Sign answer to prayer received by Susanne and me in the summer of 1995, along with several other visits of the holy Spirit and Jesus perceived by Susanne during illness and surgical recoveries and later tests for Alzheimer's, gave us comfort and assurance of God's presence, and hope that Susanne was going to be safe in God's loving arms in heaven, in a better place, one day and that we would enjoy a wonderful reunion there, This assurance also helped me to care for Susanne over the many sad days of those years.

Isaiah had it right about Jesus as our savior, as quoted in Isaiah 9:6–7(NIV):

> "For to us a child is born, to us a son is given, and the government will be on his shoulders.
>
> And he will be called Wonderful Counselor, Mighty God, Everlasting Father, Prince of Peace.
>
> Of the increase of his government and peace there will be no end. He will reign on David's throne and over his kingdom, establishing and upholding it with justice and righteousness from that time on and forever.
>
> The zeal of the LORD Almighty will accomplish this."

A Closing Prayer from King David, the Psalmist:

Psalm 71: 15-19 (NIV)

"My mouth will tell of your righteousness,

Of your salvation all day long,

Though I know not its measure.

I will come and proclaim your mighty acts,

O sovereign Lord;

I will proclaim your righteousness, yours alone.

Since my youth, O God, you have taught me, and

To this day I declare your marvelous deeds.

Even when I am old and gray, do not forsake me, O God,

Till I declare your power to the next generation,

Your might to all who are to come.

Your righteousness reaches to the skies, O God,

You who have done great things.

Amen

David B. Blanco

AUTHOR'S ADDITIONAL COMMENTS ABOUT MIRACULOUS SIGNS

---

1. A prophecy of Jesus or prediction of the future uttered by Him at His trial before the Sanhedrin, as set forth in Matthew 26:57-64(NIV), may have been fulfilled in earlier times, as well as in our time in the Cloud Sign, which was captured in the photograph shown above.

In Matthew 26:57, Jesus is taken before Caiaphas, the high priest where the teachers of the law and the elders had assembled. The chief priests and the whole Sanhedrin were looking for false evidence to condemn Jesus to death. Two men declared that Jesus had said, "I am able to destroy the temple of God and build it in three days."

Caiaphas said to Jesus, "What is it that these men are testifying against you?" But Jesus was silent. Caiaphas said, "I charge you under oath by the living God: Tell us if you are the Christ, the Son of God."

Jesus said, "Yes, you have said so. But I tell you: In the future you will see the *Son of Man sitting at the right hand of the Mighty One and coming on the clouds of heaven.*"

Then the high priest tore his clothes and said, "He has uttered blasphemy! Why do we need any more witnesses? Look, now you have now heard the blasphemy. What is your judgment?"

They answered, "He deserves death." Then they spat in His face and struck Him and some slapped Him, saying, "Prophesy to us, Christ. Who hit you?"

One could argue that this prophecy of Jesus has become fulfilled by the Cloud Sign, made by God's angel. There is no telling how many times this Cloud Sign or a variation of it has appeared to others in answer to prayer, or for other reasons. But is there a record of it?

2. It can be argued that the Cloud Sign photograph shown in this book offers convincing evidence that the God we worship is indeed a Christian God, based on two particular aspects of the Cloud Sign:.

> (A) The angel of God, who appears to have shaped the Cloud Sign into a massive *crown*, has included a face in the clouds depicted or positioned at what is symbolically "the right hand of God". The position of Christ at God's right hand after His resurrection

was forecast above by Jesus Himself and has been acknowleged numerous times in other Biblical and canonical literature; it is the place of highest honor in God's heaven or firmament. This feature of the Cloud Sign arguably confirms those sources.

(B) The dark image on the bottom right of the Cloud Sign appears to be a depiction of the episode told in Luke 8:22–25(NIV), when Jesus was asleep in the boat and a ferocious storm came up. The boat was filling with water, and Jesus' disciples were terrified. Jesus awoke and calmed the storm. And the fears of his disciples, and gave them His peace.

APPENDIX: CLOUDS, ANGELS AND CROWNS IN THE BIBLE

The Bible includes a number of references to miracles, signs, and appearances in the clouds as well as, of course, regarding angels and crowns. These references appear in the Old Testament as well as the New Testament. See the following verses:

A. Clouds

Exodus 13:21	and the Lord went before them by day in a pillar of a cloud to guide them
Isaiah 19:1	See, the Lord rides on a swift cloud.

Luke 21:27	and then they will see the Son of Man is coming in a cloud with power and great glory.
Revelation 14:14	Then I looked and lo, a white cloud, and seated on the cloud was one like a Son of Man, with a golden crown on His head …
Deuteronomy 33:26	There is none like God … who rides through the heavens to your help and on the clouds, in his majesty.
Psalm 68:4	extol him who rides upon the clouds; his name is the Lord, exult before him.
Psalm 104:3	He makes the cloud his chariot
Proverbs 25:14	like clouds and wind without rain

Daniel 7:13	I saw in the night visions, and behold, with the clouds of heaven there came one like a Son of Man, and he came to the Ancient of Days and was presented before him, and to him was given *dominion* and glory and *kingdom*, that all people … should serve him; his dominion is everlasting and shall not pass away, and his *kingdom* one that shall not be destroyed.
Matthew 24:30	… then will appear the sign of the Son of Man in heaven, with great glory and they will see the Son of Man coming on the clouds of heaven.
Matthew 26:64	I tell you, hereafter you will see the Son of Man seated at the right hand of Power and coming on the clouds of heaven.

Mark 13:26	and then they will see the Son of Man coming in clouds with great power and glory.
Mark 13:27	and then he will send out the angels, and gather his elect from the four winds, from the ends of the earth to the ends of heaven.
1 Thessalonians 4:17	Then we who are alive, who are left, shall be caught up together with them in the clouds to meet the Lord in the air.

B. Angels

Genesis 16:7	The angel of the Lord found Hagar
Genesis 22:11	But the angel of the Lord called out
Exodus 23:20	Behold, I am sending an angel ahead of you …
Numbers 22:23	When the donkey saw the angel
Judges 2:1	The angel of the Lord went up
Judges 6:22	Gideon realized that it was the angel
Judges 13:15	Manoah said to the angel of the Lord
2 Samuel 24:16	The angel of the Lord was there
1 Kings 19:7	The angel of the Lord came back
2 Kings 19:35	That night the angel of the Lord went
Psalm 34:7	The angel of the Lord encamps
Hosea 12:4	He struggled with the angel

Matthew 2:13	Behold, an angel of the Lord appeared to Joseph: take the child to Egypt for Herod is about to search for the child …
Matthew 28:2	and behold, there was a great earthquake for an angel of the Lord descended from heaven and rolled back the stone, and sat upon it. His appearance was like lightning and his raiment white as snow.
Luke 1:26	God sent the angel Gabriel
Luke 2:9	An angel of the Lord appeared to them, and the glory of the Lord shone around them, and they were filled with fear. And the angel said to them: "Be not afraid; for behold I bring you good news of a great joy which will come to all the people; for to you is born this day in the city of David a savior, who is Christ the Lord …

Luke 22:43	An angel from heaven appeared to him strengthening him.
Acts 6:15	His face was like the face of an angel (Stephen before the council)
Acts 12:7	Suddenly an angel of the Lord appeared to Peter (in prison) and helped him escape
2 Corinthians 11:14	Satan himself masquerades as an angel
Galatians 1:8	or an angel from heaven should preach
Psalm 91:11	command his angels concerning you
Matthew 4:6	command his angels concerning you
Matthew 13:39	of the age, and the harvesters are angels
Matthew 13:49	The angels will come and separate
Matthew 18:10	For I tell you that their angels
Matthew 25:41	prepared for the devil and his angels

Luke 4:10	command his angels concerning you
Luke 20:36	for they are like the angels
1 Corinthians 6:3	you not know that we will judge angels?
1 Corinthians 13:1	If I speak in the tongues of men and of angels, but have not love, I am a noisy gong.
Colossians 2:18	and the worship of angels disqualify you
Hebrews 1:4	as much superior to the angels
Hebrews 1:6	"Let all God's angels worship him."
Hebrews 1:7	"He makes his angels winds.
Hebrews 1:14	Are not all angels ministering spirits
Hebrews 2:7	made him a little lower than the angels
Hebrews 2:9	was made a little lower than the angels
Hebrews 13:2	some people have entertained angels

1 Peter 1:12	Even angels long to look
2 Peter 2:4	For if God did not spare angels
Jude v. 6	angels who did not keep their positions

C. Crown

Isa	51:11	everlasting joy will *c* their heads.
	61:3	to bestow on them a *c* of beauty
	62:3	You will be a *c* of splendor
Eze	16:12	and a beautiful *c* on your head.
Zec	9:16	like jewels in a *c*.
Mt	27:29	and then twisted together a *c* of thorns
Mk	15:17	then twisted together a *c* of thorns
Jn	19:2	The soldiers twisted together a *c*
	19:5	When Jesus came out wearing the *c*
1 Corinthians	9:25	it to get a *c* that will last forever.
	9:25	it to get a *c* that will not last;
Php	4:1	and long for, my joy and *c*,
1 Th	2:19	or the *c* in which we will glory
2 Ti	2:5	he does not receive the victor's *c*
	4:8	store for me the *c* of righteousness,
Jas	1:12	he will receive the *c*

1 Pe	5:4	You will receive the crown
Rev	2:10	and I will give you the *c* of life.
	3:11	so that no one will take your *c*.
	14:14	a son of man" with a *c* of gold

CROWNED* (CROWN)

Ps	8:5	and *c* him with glory and honor.
Pr	14:18	the prudent are *c* with knowledge.
SS	3:11	crown with which his mother *c* him
Heb	2:7	you *c* him with glory and honor
	2:9	now *c* with glory and honor

CROWNS (CROWN)

Ps	103:4	and *c* me with love and compassion
	149:4	he *c* the humble with salvation.
Pr	11:26	blessing *c* him who is willing to sell.
Rev	4:4	and had *c* of gold on their heads.
	4:10	They lay their *c* before the throne
	12:3	ten horns and seven *c* on his heads.
	19:12	and on his head are many *c*.

GLOSSARY OF KEY TERMS

Here are dictionary definitions for several important terms used in this book:

A. *Miracle*

1. "An event that appears unexplainable by the laws of nature and so is held to be supernatural in origin or an act of God" (*Webster's Dictionary* (©1985), def. 1).

2. "An extraordinary event manifesting divine intervention in human affairs" (*Merriam–Webster's Collegiate Dictionary*, 10th ed., def. 1 [hereafter "*Webster's*, 10th ed.]).

B. *Sign*

"Something material or external that stands for or signifies something spiritual" (*Webster's*, 10th ed., def. 6a).

C. *Wonder*

"A cause of astonishment" [def. 1a]; "a miracle" [1b]; "rapt attention or astonishment at something awesomely mysterious or new to one's experience" [3a] (*Webster's*, 10th ed.).

D. *Prophecy*

"A prediction"; "the inspired utterance of a prophet, viewed as a declaration of divine will"; "such a revelation transmitted orally or in writing."

E. *Prophesy*

"To reveal the will or message of God"; "to predict the future"; "to speak as a prophet."

AUTHOR'S FURTHER STATEMENTS ABOUT THE BOOK

A. I titled the book *The Cloud Sign Miracle* because I believe the Cloud Sign was a miracle captured on film by my Canon thirty-five millimeter camera in 1995, before digital cameras. (See definition of "Miracle" in Glossary of Key Terms above). These photographs of an angel preparing a cloud as a sign asked for in prayer are miraculous. They certainly are not "explainable by the laws of nature". This is clearly an "extraordinary event which seems to manifest divine intervention in human affairs." I think the cloud sign is a "sign" asked for in prayer by a living human being—delivered to that human being (and others) in a beautiful, kindly, fatherly, supernatural way, by what appears to be an angel. To my knowledge, such an event has not been reported or captured on film since the invention of film processes.

B. This book is a true story of a miraculous answer to a human prayer for a sign from God and for direction and peace in the midst of indecision, stress, worry, and anxiety.

In these events, which actually happened in my life, I received what I believe was a miraculous answer to my sincere and fervent prayer to God for personal direction at a difficult time in my life. The answer to prayer was "a sign and a wonder" created by a seraphim angel in a huge cumulus cloud in the form of a massive crown. This Cloud Sign also contained or depicted some images that were fulfillments of aspects of Jesus' life on earth and His early ministry, as well as one distinct prophecy that Jesus forecast to the Sanhedrin in His "trial" there.

C. I believe that the advice from God to me was to "seek first God's kingdom and his righteousness, and all these things shall be added unto you". See Matthew 6:33 (KJV) a verse from the Sermon on the Mount. Divine, fatherly advice for all of us.

Further Comments about the Included Photographs

The *first photo* included in the body of the book is the next-to-last photograph taken that afternoon or evening at the beach. I believe it shows the seraphim angel hard at work on the final

Cloud Sign, with the angel's face turned away from the camera's viewpoint and with the angel's back showing. The angel appears to be holding a rod and is working on the image of a face in the cloud. It appears that the face has a large brow and deep-set eyes, both of which make the face look somewhat foreboding or possibly judgmental. When this photo is compared to the second photo, which is the finished Cloud Sign, this face is seen to have moved up on the crown to the highest point of honor (on the right hand of the Father). Also, the face has become less foreboding or angry and is *not* judgmental at all. Thus, it more accurately depicts the face of Jesus, who does not judge us while we are alive on this earth, but, having been human Himself, He understands us and He forgives us our trespasses to the extent we forgive the trespasses of other people against us.

Also, there is the dark image in the bottom right of the crown, which I have described as a depiction of Jesus standing in the disciples' boat, quieting the raging storm and calming the fears of the disciples, bringing peace to the disciples, which was described in Luke 8:22–25 (NIV). Please note that after Jesus rebuked the wind and the raging waters, and the storm subsided, and all was calm, He asked his disciples: "Where is your faith?" Like us, the disciples did not trust that Jesus would "save them" though He was there with them.

The *second photo*, showing a relatively finished huge crown, has the face of Jesus, arguably, located in the top left of the crown (the right hand of God). The cloud is more obviously in the shape of a crown, and the seraphim angel has now turned around to face the camera. The angel has opened its six wings, as if the angel has nothing to hide. The angel seems to be looking at the camera openly, as if to convey, as I said in the main part of this book: "Behold! There—you have the *sign* you prayed for and your answer to prayer."

The *third photo* is one I took as a tourist a couple of years later in the Hagia Sophia Cathedral in Istanbul. To me, this photo was also a revelation, since its depiction of a seraphim angel was so very similar in appearance to the angel in the Cloud Sign photograph. The seraphim angel depicted on the ceiling of the cathedral was put there more than a thousand years ago. The similarity of the cathedral's seraphim angel depiction to the seraphim angel captured in the Cloud Sign photograph is striking. This seems to confirm the reality of this angel captured in the photograph of the ocean scene. The angel was alive and doing the will of God to answer the prayer. I believe this is profound confirmation that this Cloud Sign was indeed a true, real sign from God, by His angel, in answer to my prayer.

Made in the USA
Columbia, SC
01 October 2022